From my kitchen to yours

In the kitchen with Reese
"A True Southern Bell"
Cookbook 2

Gotham Books
30 N Gould St.
Ste. 20820, Sheridan, WY 82801
https://gothambooksinc.com/

Phone: 1 (307) 464-7800

© 2023 Teresa Burnett. All rights reserved.

No part of this book may be reproduced, stored in a retrieval system, or transmitted by any means without the written permission of the author.

Published by Gotham Books (January 26, 2023)

ISBN: 979-8-88775-201-3 (sc)
ISBN: 979-8-88775-202-0 (e)

Because of the dynamic nature of the Internet, any web addresses or links contained in this book may have changed since publication and may no longer be valid.

The views expressed in this work are solely those of the author and do not necessarily reflect the views of the publisher, and the publisher hereby disclaims any responsibility for them.

Introduction

"The Southern Bell" will take you on a journey through the South with homemade delicious recipes that comes straight from the heart to please the mouth. All recipes can be altered to your liking. And I strongly suggest all dishes be prepped in advance to assure easy cooking. This cookbook includes more of the traditional southern foods such as fatback & ham hocks. All dishes are inspired from recipes cooked by my mom, aunts, sisters, & a special loving lady whom we all loved, respected & enjoyed, my mom's best friend "Mrs. Ora D. Sigers". These dishes were cooked by each of these lovely ladies as I was growing up in the dirty ole south in my home town "Brantley, Alabama".

Table of Contents

Chicken & Dressing 1

Home-made chicken broth 3

Crackling cornbread 5

Fried cornbread/Hoecakes/Johnnycakes 7

Chicken & dumplings 9

Fried chicken livers 11

Chicken livers smothered in onions & home-made gravy 13

Home-made chicken gravy 13

Glazed baked ham w/pineapple slices & cherries 15

Fried pork chops 17

Pig feet 19

Pork neckbones & potatoes 21

Yellow rice 23

Jag rice 25

Fluffy white rice 27

Old fashion tomato rice w/fresh neckbones 29

Baked sweet potatoes wedges 31

Cabbages w/bacon 33

Green beans w/potatoes & bacon 35

Fried okra 37

Fried corn 39

Southern style collard greens w/smoked ham-hocks & okra 41

Fried squash 43

Mustard & turnips greens 45

Southern style black-eye peas 47

Rutabagas 49

Biography 51

Chicken & Dressing

Directions:

Chicken pieces cooked-giblets, thighs, legs

Cornbread-crumbled

1 can of cream of chicken

3 garlic cloves-chopped

2 onions-diced

4 stalks of celery-diced

1 large green bell pepper-diced

2 eggs

1 stick of butter melted

Chicken broth

Preheat oven to 350 and place a cast iron skillet or baking dish of your choice in the oven along with the stick of butter and let it melt. Remove skillet/baking dish from the oven and set it aside. In a large bowl add cornbread and crumble it using your fingers. Add cream of chicken, garlic, onions, celery, green peppers and eggs to the cornbread mixture. Gradually start incorporating the broth 2 cups at a time to the cornbread and try not to make the cornbread mixture too watery. If the mixture is too watery it will take hours to cook and for the middle to set. Remove the chicken from the bones using your fingers and shred it as much as you can. Add the shredded chicken to the cornbread mixture and ½ of the melted butter from the cast iron and mix well. Continue adding more broth if needed to get the consistency of pancake batter. Not too thick and not to watery. Make sure the bottom of the skillet is well coated with the butter before adding mixture. Pour dressing mixture in the skillet and bake for 35-40 minutes or until golden brown around the edge and the middle is set and not jiggling. Rotate the skillet after 20 minutes of cooking. Yields 8 or more servings.

Chicken broth recipe follows below:

HOME-MADE CHICKEN BROTH

Directions:

1 lb of each chicken giblets-livers, gizzards,

Chicken-3 thighs, 3 legs, chicken fats, chicken bones

1¼ cup of chicken base

1 tsp of salt

1 tsp of salt-free seasonings

1 tsp of ground ginger

1 tsp of black pepper

1 tbsp of black pepper corns

2 tbsp of onion powder

2 tbsp of garlic powder

½ of an onion

1 tbsp of dried chopped onions

1 tbsp of dried parsley

1 celery stalk cut in half

1½ gallon of cold water

Place a large stock pot on top of the stove. Add chicken, water along with all the ingredients. Bring to a heavy boil, then reduce to a low simmer. Skim off all the scum that foams to the top surface and 86 it (get rid of). Allow everything to slow cook for 4 hours, removing the chicken & livers after 1 hour and gizzards after 2 hours. Once chicken has cooled enough remove it from the bones and place the bones back into the pot and continue cooking for the remainder couple of hours. When done stock will be reduced to about 1 gallon. Chicken broth can be used for numerous of cooking. Use what you need and freeze the rest. Yields: 1 gallon

CRACKLING CORNBREAD

Directions:

1¼ cup of self-rising cornmeal

¼ cup of self-rising flour

¾ cup of buttermilk plus ¼ cup more if needed

1 egg

¼ cup of oil divided in half

½ lb of pork crackling skins broken in pieces

Preheat oven to 350. Add cracklings to a sheet pan and place them in the oven. Cook them for 2-3 minutes, long enough for cracklings to release some of it's natural oils and to cook out some of the rawness of the cracklings. In a medium bowl add cornmeal, flour and egg then slowly start incorporating the buttermilk, and half of the oil. Add cracklings and its oil then stir all ingredients together until everything is all incorporated and batter is smooth. Pour the remaining oil in the skillet and make sure the bottom of the skillet is well coated, then pour the batter in the skillet. Bake for 30-35 minutes till golden brown. Serve hot. Yields 5-6 servings.

Fried cornbread/Hoecakes/Johnnycakes

Directions:

1 cup of self rising cornmeal

2 tbsp of self rising flour

1 tbsp of sugar-optional

1 egg

1 tbsp of oil

¾-1 cup of buttermilk

Oil for frying

Syrup-optional

Add the first 4 ingredients in a bowl then gradually start incorporating the buttermilk a little at a time. Mix until you have a smooth batter similar to hush-puppies batter. A little on the thicker side than a cornbread batter. Set it aside. Try not to make the batter too loose or liquidity. In case it is a little loose, just add a tad more cornmeal. Place a cast iron skillet or any skillet you have on hand, on top of the stove and add ¼ cup of oil on medium heat. As soon as the oil is hot, drop ¼ cup of batter into the hot oil. Drop 3-4 hoecakes at a time. Do not overcrowd the skillet. Fry them in batches if needed. Spoon the batter in the oil as if you're making mini pancakes. Fry till golden brown about 2-3 minutes each side. Add a little oil if needed after each frying. When done drain on paper towel. Serve hot with a little syrup over each. Yields: 8 hoecakes.

Chicken & dumplings

Directions:
1½ lbs of chicken legs, wings, thighs, gizzards, hearts, chicken necks & livers
Chicken broth/water
½ cup of cream of chicken
2 chicken flavored bouillon packets or cubes
Salt to taste or seasonings of your choice
Black pepper to taste

Dumplings

3 cups of self rising flour
1 cup of milk
1½ stick of cold butter cut in small chunks
½ stick of whole butter

Add flour and butter together in a large bowl and begin working them together either by using your fingers or a fork. Work them together until dough starts to look crumbly and you can see little specks of butter. Gradually start adding milk a little at a time and mix together until it is coming together as if you're making biscuits. Mix until everything has come together and there's nothing left in the bowl. You should have a smooth dough ball. Cover and refrigerate to let the dough become firm. About 30 minutes up to 1 hour. When ready scatter some flour around on a clean cutting board and lay the dough. Cut in 4 sections to make 4 balls. Use a rolling pin, coat it with flour. Begin rolling it as flat as it will get and as long as it will go. Rotating dough around. Take a pizza cutter and go up and down making multiple lines, then make multiple lines going sideways. Cut until you have either squares or rectangle shape dumplings. Repeat same procedures with the rest of the dough. Add chicken and it's giblets along with broth and seasonings to a large pan and bring up to a high boil, skim off any fats then reduce heat to low. Cover pot and let the chicken and giblets slow cook for 1 hour. Remove chicken and giblets from the liquid and let them cool down, and then shred as much meat off the bones as you can and place it back into the same pot. Increase heat to a boil and add cream of chicken, stir it around to incorporate. Begin adding dumplings. When dumplings are dropped they will swell and rise to the top. Let them cook on medium heat covered for 20-25 minutes or until the dumplings has fallen to the bottom and no longer looking raw or doughy. Once dumplings has dropped to the bottom, stir them to keep them from sticking. When done add ½ stick of butter and let it melt completely in the dumplings. Adjust seasonings if needed. Yields: plenty

For 1 dumpling ball I used 3 cups of broth along with some shredded chicken and giblets for a serving of 4 or more.

Fried chicken livers

Directions:

1 lb of chicken livers

Salt to taste

Black pepper to taste

1-2 cups of flour

Oil for frying

Rinse livers under cold water and place them in a strainer to rid extra water and then lay them on paper towels and pat dry. Add oil and heat it up to a deep skillet, pot, or deep fryer. Add flour and seasonings to a paper, or Ziploc bag and add livers. Shake the bag and make sure they are all coated with the flour. Remove them from the bag and lay each on a rack and let them sit for 3-4 minutes so the flour can adhere to the livers. Once oil has heated up begin dropping the livers, a few pieces at a time. Do not over crowd the frying process, fry in batches if needed. Let them cook for 4-5 minutes. Serve them with any sauce of your choice. Ranch & hot sauce is an excellent dipping sauce for these. Serve hot. Yields: 3-4 servings.

Chicken livers smothered in onions & home-made gravy

Home-made chicken gravy

Directions:

3 tbsp of oil or the brown bits left at the bottom of the pan after frying chicken

3 tbsp of flour

1 onion-sliced

4-5 cups of chicken broth

¼ tsp of chicken flavored bouillon base

Black pepper to taste

¼ tsp of garlic powder

¼ tsp of onion powder

¼ tsp of garlic & herb seasoning

¼ tsp of salt-free seasoning

Add oil to a cast iron skillet or a frying pan and place it on top of the stove on medium heat. Add onions and saute for 1 minute and then add flour. Use a whisk or wooden spoon to stir until it begins to look like a paste. Gradually start incorporating the broth and whisking to keep gravy from lumping up. Do not add all the broth at once. Add as much as you need to begin the thickening started then add bouillons and seasonings. Once gravy has started thickening reduce heat and let it simmer on low heat for 10 minutes without interfering with it. The longer the gravy cooks it will continue to thicken, add more broth as needed. Adjust seasoning and serve. Serve hot. And over a bead of rice or mash potatoes. Yields: plenty

Glazed Baked Ham w/Pineapple Slices & Cherries

Directions:

1-butt portion ham or shank

¼ cup of brown sugar

2 tbsp of honey

½ tsp of yellow mustard

4 oz can of sliced pineapples

Maraschinos cherries

Cooking spray

Preheat oven to 350. To get rid of some of the salt in the ham. Rinse ham and place it in a pot big enough to hold it along with enough cold water to reach the ham about half way. Let it come to a high boil, and then reduce it down to a medium boil. Let ham boil for 3 minutes each side, totaling 12 minutes. Remove ham from the boiling water and place it on paper towels to drain any extra water. And then place the ham on a baking sheet pan lined with aluminum foil. Insert 5-6 toothpicks in the ham and place the pineapples and cherries on each. Place a small pot on top of the stove and add brown sugar, honey, mustard, and enough juice from the pineapples to dissolve the brown sugar. Cook everything together on medium heat so that the glaze can begin to start bubbling and reducing down to a syrupy consistency, approximately 1-2 minutes. Cut crosshatch patterns in the fat on the ham. Brush the glaze all over the ham and spray it all over with cooking spray, then place it in the oven. Bake for 30-35 minutes, rotating it around to get even cooking all around and pineapples and cherries have begin to get a little charred on them. Brush any extra glaze over the ham or when sliced drizzle it what's left all on it. Wait a few minutes before slicing to allow the juices to settle in. Yields: a lot

Fried pork chops

Directions:

1-2 lbs of pork chops

¼ tsp of salt

¼ tsp of black pepper

¼ tsp of garlic powder

¼ tsp of onion powder

¼ tsp of turmeric

1 tsp of salt-free seasonings

¼ tsp of garlic & herb seasoning

2½-3 cups self- rising flour

Oil

Add flour to a paper or plastic bag and set it aside. Rinse pork chops under cool water and place them on paper towel to get rid of the excess water. Place pork chops in a large bowl and add seasonings. Make sure they are well coated with seasonings and place them in the bag of flour. Shake bag to coat each pork chops and remove them from flour and lay them on a wire rack. Add oil to a deep fryer on 400 or a large pot on top of the stove to medium high heat. When oil has reached its temperature, begin adding pork chops a few pieces at a time. Once pork chops has started to really fry reduce heat to 350. Let them fry without constantly turning them. Fry till golden brown approximately 5 minutes each side. Serve hot. Yields 5 or more servings.

PIG FEET

Directions:

1-2 lbs of sliced or cut up pig feet

Meat tenderizer

½ package of Goya Sazon

Salt to taste

Black pepper to taste

1 tsp of any brand pork rub

1 tsp of turmeric

1 tsp of crushed red pepper flakes

1 heaping tbsp of vinegar

Hot sauce of your choice

Rinse pig feet under cold running water and place them in a large bowl. Season them with the meat tenderizer, half of the Sazon packet, salt, black pepper, pork rub, turmeric and crushed peppers. Using your hands work the ingredients into the pork. Add them to a large pot with just enough cold water to cover them. Place them on top of the stove on high heat, cover pot and let them come to a boil. When water begins to boil rapidly, remove lid and skim off any scum that foams. Do not stir! Add vinegar. Reduce heat to a low simmering boil, recover and let them slow cook for 2½ hours or until pig feet is tender and practically separating from the bones. Adjust seasoning and serve. Yields: 3-4 servings.

Pork neckbones & potatoes

Directions:

2 lbs of fresh pork neckbones

6 russet potatoes-peeled & diced

1 large onion-sliced

1 tbsp of salt or salt free seasoning

¼ tsp of black pepper

1 tbsp of onion powder

1 tbsp of garlic powder

¼ tsp of all-purpose seasoning

¼ tsp of meat tenderizer

¼ tsp of soul-food seasoning-optional

2 tbsp of flour

Clean neckbones and place them in a large pot and season them with all the seasonings. Place pot on top of the stove and add just enough water to cover the neckbones. Cover pot and bring up to a boil then reduce heat to a low simmering boil. Remove any scum that foams to the surface. Cook neckbones for 35 minutes. Remove 1/3 cup of broth and let it cool then add onions and potatoes. Allow everything to come back up to a boil. Once broth has cooled add flour to make a slurry thicken and set it aside. then add onions and potatoes. Once the potatoes and neckbones has begin to come up to a boil add slurry mix and reduce heat to a medium to low simmering boil. Cover pot and continue to cook for 15-20 more minutes to allow the pot liquids to begin to thicken, and potatoes are getting folk tender. Adjust seasonings and serve hot. For a beautiful presentation serve with cornbread, green scallions & cracked black pepper. Yields: 4 or more servings.

YELLOW RICE

Directions:

¼ tsp of Goya Sazon seasoning (Con Azafran)-yellow top package

¼ tsp of turmeric

1½ tbsp any Adobo seasoning

Salt to taste-optional

½ tsp of black pepper

1 chicken flavored bouillon cubes or packet

1½ tbsp of garlic powder

2 tbsp of Sofrito

1½ tbsp of oil

2 cups long grain rice rinsed

3 ½ cups of chicken broth or water

Add Sazon, Adobo, turmeric, salt, bouillons, rice, garlic powder, Sofrito and olive oil to a rice pan or heavy bottom pot. Stir everything together till all is coated with the Sazon, and the rice has turned a bright orange color. Add chicken broth or water and bring to a boil on medium high. Allow rice to come to a boil so most of the liquids can begin evaporating. Once liquid has almost evaporated cover pot with aluminum foil and a tight fitting lid. Reduce heat to low and let rice cook without interfering for 15 minutes. Remove foil lid then stir rice, recover and cook for 10 more minutes or until rice is done to your liking. Leave covered until ready to serve. Serve hot. Yields 5-6 servings.

JAG RICE
In loving memory of Margaret A. Jones

Directions:

2 tbsp of oil

½ of a red bell pepper-diced

½ of an onion-diced

½ lb of ground beef

Salt to taste

¼ tsp of Black pepper

¼ tsp of garlic powder

¼ tsp of onion powder

¼ tsp of herb seasonings-any

1 package of beef bouillon or 1 beef bouillon cube

2½ cups of rice

Beef broth

Add a medium rice pan or heavy pot on top of stove and add oil on medium high heat. Saute the peppers, and onions just enough to get the aroma of the onions, peppers and the onions are not turning brown around the edges. Add ground beef and seasonings. Cook the beef till is no longer bright red. A little red is OK as it will finish cooking when all ingredients are added and cooking is continuing. When done drain oil from ground-beef and add it back on top of the stove in the same pot. Add the rice and gradually start incorporating the broth a little a time. Do not add all the broth at once; only add enough to cover the rice and over by a ½ inch. Bring to a medium high boil and allow most of the broth to evaporate. Cover pot with aluminum foil and a tight fitting lid and cook for 15 minutes on low heat. Leaving it alone without constant interference. After the 15 minutes are up, remove the foil and lid. Stir the rice around and recover. Continue cooking it for another 5-10 minutes or until rice is completely done. Adjust seasoning. Serve hot. Yields 5-6 or more servings

FLUFFY WHITE RICE

Directions:

2 tbsp of oil

¼ tsp of salt or to taste

¼ tsp of black or white pepper

2 cups of rice

3 cups of cold water

Add water to a heavy bottom rice pan or pot and bring it up to a high boil then add oil, salt and rice. Once everything has came up to a boil, allow most of the water to evaporate. Cover pot with aluminum foil and a tight fitting lid. Cook for 15 minutes and then remove lid and foil. Fluff rice with a folk and recover. Let it continue cooking for 5-10 more minutes or until rice is completely done. Do not continue to stir or mix the rice. Too much stirring will make the rice become gummy or as we call it! soggy rice. Yields: 4-5 servings

Old Fashion Tomato Rice w/Fresh Neckbones

Directions:

½ lb of fresh neck bones
½ tbsp of garlic powder
¼ tsp of garlic & herb seasoning
¼ tsp of soul-food seasoning-optional
¼ tsp of all purpose seasoning
¼ tsp of salt-optional
¼ tsp of black pepper
1-14.5 oz can of diced tomatoes
1 heaping tbsp of tomato paste
1 tomato & chicken flavored bouillon cube
2 cups of rice
Beef broth or water

Rinse neckbones and place them in a large pot along with the seasonings then add enough broth/water to just barely covering the meat. Bring up to a boil and skim off any scum that foams to the top surface, and reduce heat to a low simmering boil. Allow neckbones to cook for 35-40 minutes or until they are becoming very tender. Remove them from the liquid and allow them to cool and remove as much of the meat as you can from the neckbones. Or just leave them whole as they are. Add dice tomatoes and it's juices, tomato paste, and bouillon to the pot and let it come up to a boil. Add the meat, rice and stir it around in the liquid. Leave uncovered to allow some of the liquid to evaporate. Reduce heat to a low setting. Cover rice with a piece of aluminum foil and it's lid. Continue cooking for 15 minutes without meddling, remove lid and foil and stir rice around. Recover and continue cooking for 5-10 more minutes or until completely done. Yields 4-5 or more servings.

Vegetarian Option:

Add oil to a rice pot or any heavy bottom pot and turn on heat. Add tomatoes, bouillon, tomato sauce/paste. Cook till sauce is looking like a paste. Add seasonings & rice. Mix all ingredients together so that the rice is incorporated & covered in the sauce, then add 3 cups of vegetable broth/water, or just enough to cover the rice.

Baked sweet potatoes wedges

Directions:

4 sweet potatoes

½ tsp of oil

2 tbsp of butter

1 tbsp of brown sugar

1 tbsp of honey

Preheat oven to 350. Rinse potatoes in cool running water and place them on paper towels to dry. Cut potatoes in wedges and place them in a large bowl. Drizzle the oil all over the potatoes. Using your hands make sure the oil is coating each potatoes. Line a baking sheet pan with aluminum foil and lay each potato. Add them to the preheated oven and bake for 15 minutes. While the potatoes are baking, let's make some glaze for our potatoes. Add butter to a small pan and let it melt on low heat then add the brown sugar & honey. Mix them together so the brown sugar can began to dissolve and the mixture can start bubbling. After the 15 minutes remove the potatoes from the oven and add them to the pot of hot mixture and fold or toss them in the brown sugar mixture. Make sure the glaze is completely covering the potatoes. Add them back to the pan and back in the oven to continue cooking for the remaining 5 minutes, or until tender when pricked with a folk. Feel free to peel the sweet potatoes before baking. Rotate pan and turn sweet potatoes on the opposite side to get that charred look. Serve hot. Yields 4 or more servings.

CABBAGES W/BACON

Directions:

1 head of cabbage-any size

4-5 slices of bacon-cut in half

¼ cup of extra bacon drippings or oil

Salt to taste

Black pepper to taste

1 tsp of crushed red pepper-optional

Water or vegetable broth

½ lb of whole or cut okra

½ of an onion-sliced

Cut cabbage in half and then cut in half again until there are 4 halves, remove cores and begin cutting or chopping the cabbage. Cabbage doesn't have to be cut or chop perfect there's no particular way to cut it. Place cut cabbages in a strainer or colander and rinse under cold water and set them aside. Cut bacon in ½ and place it in the pan and cook it long enough to get some of the bacon fat, and it begins to wilt about 2-3 minutes. Add cabbages, bacon drippings and oil, salt, black pepper, crush red pepper and 2 cups of cold water. Let it come up to a boil and then cover. No need to add lots of water since cabbage makes the majority of its own water. Cover and cook for 30-35 minutes or till tender to your taste. Add okra and onions the last 10 minutes of cooking. Adjust season and serve. Yields 5-6 or more servings

When cooking cabbage use only meats that will not change the color of the cabbage. For example smoke meats will turn cabbage a dark color. Use meats such as bacon, ham-bone, pig tails, fatback or salt pork. And be sure to cook salt pork before adding to the cabbages. It's extremely salty and needs to be cooked first to remove the majority of the salt. Discard salty water and add cabbage with fresh cold water.

Green beans w/potatoes & bacon

Directions:

3 medium to large potatoes

1-2 lbs of fresh green beans

4 slices of bacon

2 tbsp of oil or bacon grease

1 small onion-slice

¼ tsp of salt

½ tsp of cracked black pepper

1 tsp of garlic & herb seasonings

¼ tsp of garlic powder

¼ tsp of onion powder

¼ tsp of soul-food seasonings-optional

Peel potatoes and cut them in chunks then add them to a medium pot along with salt and cold water. Let potatoes come to a boil then reduce heat to a medium low. Covered pot and cook potatoes for 5 minutes. In case the water starts to boil over while covered, tilt the cover ½ ways. While potatoes are cooking cut bacon in half and add 2 tbsp of oil and saute for 1-2 minutes, just long enough to get the bacon grease and the bacon is not getting crispy then set aside. Drain potatoes and add them back to the same pan, then add green beans, onions, seasonings, bacon and it's drippings along with 1 cup of vegetable stock or cold water. Bring pot to a boil then reduce heat to low, cover pot to allow everything to cook together for 5-10 minutes. Adjust seasonings and serve hot. Yields 4-5 servings

Green beans can be cooked and flavored with other meats such as a leftover ham bone, smoke ham hocks, or for non pork eaters smoke turkey.

Fried okra

Directions:

1-2 lbs of cut okra-fresh or frozen

1 cup of cornmeal

2 heaping tbsp of self-rising flour

   Salt to taste

   Black pepper to taste

1 egg white

Oil-for frying

Add cornmeal, flour, salt and black pepper to a small plastic or brown paper bag and set it aside. Add egg to a bowl and beat it then add to the okra. Make sure okra gets well coated with the egg and set it aside. On medium heat add oil to a deep skillet or deep fryer with a basket, and turn on heat. Add okra to cornmeal mixture and shake bag to coat all over. Remove okra from cornmeal mixture and lay them on a wire rack or whatever you have to place them. Once oil has heated up to its appropriate temperature begin adding okra. Fry in batches if needed. Be careful and try not to cause a splatter from the oil. It can cause serious burns and blisters. Fry okra until you have a golden brown crust. Okra will usually float to the top when it is ready. Approximately 3-5 minutes. Drain on paper towel. Serve hot. Yields 4-5 servings

Fried corn

Directions:

1½ stick of butter

6 ears of corn shucked and cut off the cob or 3-4 cans of whole kernel & 1 can of cream corn

2 tbsp of flour

Salt to taste

Black pepper to taste

1½ cup of milk

Preheat oven to 350. Place a cast iron skillet or any skillet that is oven safe on top of the stove on low heat and melt butter. In a large bowl add corn, flour and seasonings, along with a cup of the milk. Stir everything together then add the remaining ½ cup of milk. Increase heat to a medium high and pour the corn mixture in the skillet. Cook on top of the stove till a little brown crust under the bottom of the corn forms, approximately 10 minutes. Place skillet in the oven and continue cooking for 10 more minutes. Remove from oven and add more butter. Let corn sit for 5 minutes to settle. Adjust seasonings if needed. The longer the corn sits it will become thicker. Add milk to preheat.   Serve hot. Yields: 7 or more servings.

Southern style collard greens w/smoked ham-hocks & okra

Directions:

1-2 bundles of fresh collard greens-chopped and cleaned

2 lbs of smoked ham hocks or meats of your choice

Salt to taste

Black pepper to taste

1 tbsp of crushed red peppers-optional

¼ cup of oil-bacon drippings, vegetable or olive oil,

¼ tsp of baking soda

½ lb of okra

Wash and clean ham hocks and place them in a large pot, along with cold water. Bring them to a boil then reduce heat to a simmering medium low heat. Cover pot and allow them to cook slowly for 1½-2 hours, or until they are coming to the stage of tenderness and separating from the bone. Add greens in the pot with the ham hocks along with the seasonings, oil, and baking soda. Increase heat to a medium boil. Recover and continue cooking for 1 more hour. As the greens are cooking the meat will continue to get tender and fall completely off the bones. The last 10 minutes of cooking add okra, stir and continuing cooking for the remaining minutes left. Adjust seasonings if needed and serve hot. Yields 6-7 or more servings.

FRIED SQUASH

Directions:

4 medium-large squash

1 large onion-sliced thin

2 garlic cloves-chopped

3 tbsp of oil

½ tbsp of onion powder

½ tbsp of garlic powder

½ tsp of garlic & herb seasoning

1 tsp of dry parsley

¼ tsp of soul-food seasonings-optional

¼ tsp salt to taste

¼ tsp black pepper

¼ tsp of crushed red pepper flakes-optional

Rinse whole squash in cold water and cut the tips off on both ends. Slice squash in ½ inch slices or slice on a bias then place them in a large bowl, along with the onions and garlic. Season squash with the seasonings and herbs then drizzle a small amount of oil over them. Toss them around in the bowl so that the seasons is well coating them. Set them aside. Add the oil to a deep heavy bottom skillet or a Dutch oven and place it on top of the stove on medium heat. Add onions and squash to the skillet then cover and let it cook for 10 minutes. As the squash cooks it will begin to make water that's perfectly normal. Remove cover and allow squash to continue cooking until the majority of the water has evaporated, approximately 5-10 more minutes. A tad of liquor left in the squash is OK, you don't want them dry!! Adjust seasoning and serve hot. Yields 5 or more servings.

Mustard & Turnips Greens

Directions:

2 bunches of each mustard greens & turnips greens

1 lb of either ham-hocks, pig tails, or meats of your choice

¼ tsp of salt

¼ tsp of soul food seasoning

½ tbsp of black pepper

¼ tsp of crush red pepper flakes

¼ tsp of onion powder

½ tsp of baking soda

1 tbsp of white sugar

¼ cup of oil-bacon drippings, vegetable or olive oil

½ lb of whole or cut okra

1 onion-sliced

Rinse ham-hocks under cold water and place them in a large pot and add just enough cold water to cover them. Place them on top of the stove and cover pot. Bring them to a high boil then reduce heat to a medium low and let them cook slowly for 45 minutes to an hour, depending on how tender they are getting. While the ham hocks are cooking begin prepping the greens. Remove as much of the stems from the mustard and turnip greens and place them in the sink with cold water. Let them sit in the sink for about 15 minutes to loosen up the dirt and the dirt sinks to the bottom. Remove greens from the 1st water and add them to clean water, rinse them 2-3 more times and place them in either a colander or bowl and set them aside. When ham hocks are almost tender add greens and season with salt, crush red pepper flakes, baking soda, sugar and oil. Cover pot and let them cook for another 1 hours on medium heat. Do not let them boil heavy, medium to low boil is OK. Add okra & onions the last 10 minutes of cooking. Serve hot. Yields 6-7 or more servings.

Non pork eaters, substitute the pork with smoke turkey. You do not have to mix greens. Cook either alone using the same procedure. If using salt pork be sure to cook some of the salt out and 86 the water (get rid of) before adding to the greens.

Southern Style Black-Eye Peas

Directions:

1 lb bag of dry black-eye peas-soaked overnight

½ lb of pig tails

Salt to taste

Black pepper to taste

1 tbsp of sugar

2-3 tbsp of oil or bacon drippings

½ lb of okra-whole or cut

1 small to medium onion-sliced

Rinse pig tails under cold water and place them in a large pot along with just enough cold water to cover them. Bring to a boil then reduce heat to a low simmer and cook meat for 45 minutes or until almost tender. Drain peas and rinse under cold water and add them in the same pot with the pig tails along with the seasonings and oil. Increase the heat from low to a higher level to begin the boiling process then reduce it down to a medium. Add sugar, oil or bacon drippings and cover pot. Cook peas for 50 minutes or until soft. The last minute 10 minutes of cooking add okra and onions. Serve hot with white rice and cornbread. Yields 6 or more servings.

Peas can be cooked and flavored with other meats such as, smoked or fresh neck bones, ham hocks, smoke turkey, leftover ham bone, hog jowls or bacon. Adding sugar will cut the bitterness out of the peas and not make them sweet.

Rutabagas

Directions:

Rutabaga

½ lb of smoked neck bones

1 tbsp of sugar

1 tbsp of oil-bacon grease or oil of your choice

¼ tsp of salt

¼ tsp of black pepper

1 small onion-sliced thin

Add neck bones to a pot and add just enough cold water to cover them. Cover pot and bring to a boil then reduce heat to a medium to low boil. Let neck bones cook for 45-50 minutes unbothered. While the neck bones are cooking, peel and cut rutabagas in chunks and place them in a bowl of cold water and set them aside. A potato peeler is better for helping to peel the rutabaga. When neck bones are getting tender or reaching it's tender peaks, add rutabagas along with the sugar, oil, salt & pepper. Cover and let them continue to cook for 30-35 minutes or till prick with a folk they are folk tender. Add onions the last 5 minutes of cooking. Serve with hot butter crackling cornbread. Yields 4 or more servings.

Biography

Hello my name is Teresa A. Burnett. Born and raised in Brantley, Alabama. A small town where I started & finished my elementary, middle, & high school education. After graduating high school I left home and started a whole new journey of life. I moved to Worcester, Massachusetts a state where I currently reside. I worked hard & put myself through 2 different colleges, beginning with Culinary Arts graduating in April of 2004 at Salter's School, known now as Salter College. Later I enrolled in Quinsigamond Community College, where I graduated in May 2012 with a Certificate in Food Service Management. I continued my education & graduated with an Associate's degree in Science in August 2013. Throughout it all my passion has always been the love of cooking.

Teresa A. Burnett

59